A Dog Like Scruff

Written by Pat Moon
Illustrated by Lisa Smith

Harcourt
Supplemental Publishers

Rigby • Steck-Vaughn

www.steck-vaughn.com

Contents

A Scruffy Dog 3

"You Bad Dog!" 10

"Try to Be Good" 16

A Dog Like Scruff 22

A Scruffy Dog

One day, Tina and Rita found a dog.
It was sitting at their door.

"Doggy!" said Rita.

"Cool!" said Tina.

"Shoo!" said Mom.

But the dog ran in.

"She wants to be our dog," said Tina.
"Can we keep her?"

"No," said Mom. "She has a family.
Look at her tag. Her name is Scruff."
Mom looked at the dog. "I can see
why she's called Scruff," she said.

Mom called the number on Scruff's tag. No one answered, so she left a message.

Just then, Ginger meowed. Scruff was eating Ginger's dinner! "Bad dog!" said Rita.

"She wants some food," said Tina.

Mom put some food down for Scruff. "There you go, you scruffy dog," she said.

Ginger looked mad.

Then Scruff went in Ginger's bed!
"Meow!" cried Ginger.

"You bad little dog!" said Mom. "That's
Ginger's bed."

Later, Dad came home. He looked at Scruff. "Who is this?" he asked.

"It's Scruff!" said Rita.

Tina told Dad all about Scruff.

At dinner, Dad's food went missing. "Where's my food?" he asked.

Scruff was eating it! "You bad dog!" said Tina.

No one called about Scruff. Tina was pleased, but Mom was not. She put an ad in the newspaper.

"If no one calls, can I keep her?" Tina asked Mom.

"No," said Mom. "If no one calls, we'll take her to the animal shelter."

"Please!" cried Tina.

"No," said Mom. "We don't want a dog—not a scruffy, bad one like Scruff."

The next day, Scruff was very bad.
She ran off with Dad's shoe.

Later, the chicken for dinner went missing. "Where can it be?" asked Mom. Scruff and Ginger were missing, too.

The family found Scruff and Ginger in the yard. They found the chicken, too! "You bad dog!" said Dad.

"And bad Ginger, too!" said Mom.

"Look!" Tina said to Mom and Dad.
"Ginger likes Scruff now!"

"Try to Be Good"

The next day, Mom found a hole in the yard. "Oh, no!" she cried.

Dad looked down the hole. "What is that down there?" he asked.

"It's your shoe!" said Tina.

"You bad dog!" the family said to Scruff.

"Oh, Scruff," said Tina. "Please try to be good so I can keep you."

Scruff did try to be good. But she chased a cat in the yard. "You bad, scruffy dog!" Mom cried.

Scruff looked very sad. "Just don't do it again, Scruff," said Mom. She gave Scruff a little pat.

When Dad came home, Scruff jumped on him. "Look! I'm all scruffy now!" Dad cried.

Scruff licked and licked Dad. She wanted to lick him clean. Tina and Rita laughed. Mom and Dad laughed, too.

"See?" Tina asked Scruff. "They like you now! I'm going to ask again if I can keep you."

Tina went to see Mom, but Mom had bad news.

"Scruff's family just called," Mom said.
"They want to take her home."

Mom and Dad looked sad. Rita cried.
Tina cried and cried and cried.

A Dog Like Scruff

The next day, Scruff's family came and took her home. "I'm going to miss that dog," said Mom.

"Me, too," said Rita.

"Me, too!" meowed Ginger.

Dad was reading the newspaper. "Look at this," he said. "The animal shelter has lots of dogs that need good homes."

"I don't want just any dog!" said Tina. "I want Scruff!"

"Let's go and see," said Dad.

The family went to the animal shelter. They looked at the dogs.

One dog looked like a very good dog. He was eating his dinner. Another dog was a very clean dog. She was sitting down. One dog was a very scruffy dog. He was chasing his tail.

"We want that dog!" cried Tina and Rita and Mom and Dad.